Infused

26 Spa Inspired
Natural Vitamin Waters
(Cleansing Fruit Infused Water Recipe Book)

Kate Evans Scott
David Pearson

KL PRESS

This book is dedicated to everyone
who seeks to live their healthiest life.

Contents

KATE EVANS SCOTT & DAVID PEARSON

Introduction
By David Pearson

My cousin Kate and I have an unquenchable thirst for naturally infused waters. So much so, that we were talking one day about how wonderful it would be to take our favorite recipes and do something creative with them in book form.

You might think that gathering a few recipes here and there from our memories and scribbled-on napkins would be fairly simple. Strangely enough, when we sat down to collaborate for the first time, we found ourselves scratching our heads. We soon realized that our love affair with homemade vitamin water was a very organic thing. In the past, when the desire to have an infusion arose, each of us just -knew- what to whip up (usually spontaneously). So, after a few days of filtering through dozens of recipe variations, we finally settled on 26 of our most favorite and most used creations.

We hope these infusions will become staples in your healthy lifestyle as much as they have in ours! Enjoy!!

Looking Beyond the Label

Picking up a commercially made bottle of vitamin water might seem like the easiest thing to do when you're on the go and want to quench your thirst in some healthy way. The problem is, of course, that the commercially made versions of vitamin water out there are chock full of nasty ingredients like crystalline fructose, artificial colors and 'natural flavor'. Vitamin water sold in the stores is essentially glorified sugar water. Once you look beyond the snappy colors and clever labels and actually read the nutritional information on these drinks, the truth can be a little unsettling.

So, this is where homemade takes centre stage AGAIN. The beauty of making your very own vitamin water is that it is easy to do, tastes infinitely more delicious than the store brands and is actually very healthy for you. These homemade brews also encourage you to drink more water which is a huge plus given that most of us are walking around continuously dehydrated.

While most of us do see it as important, drinking more water every day (ideally 6-8 glasses) can seem like a bit of a chore. Adding a little pizzazz to your water bottle with naturally infused flavours can sometimes be enough to 'push' you to go get another refill.

Key Benefits
Of Natural Infusions:

There are a number of benefits to making your own infusions.
Some key benefits are:

- Simple
- Full of antioxidants and nutrients from the herbs and fruits
- Helps children consume more water by making it a 'fun' experience
- Gives you better control of your weight
- Ingredients can be reused
- Amazing source for vitamins and minerals
- Variety of flavors
- Energizes you
- Cleanses your body
- Rejuvenates

Sometimes it's just easier to drink something healthy than it is to eat a healthy meal. The wonderful thing about naturally infused water is that you get the best of both worlds - once you have consumed the vitamin water, you can also eat the fruits and other ingredients to take advantage of the fiber content.

Purified Water

Vs

Fluoridated Tap Water

Fluoridated water has been in the news lately because more and more people are starting to question its necessity and adverse health effects.

Reports that have been long standing which claim that fluoride helps to prevent cavities are now being questioned by researchers and medical professionals. If you do a bit of digging yourself, you'll find many new studies on the potential health risks associated with this chemical. You'll even find that the origins of water fluoridation raise some ethical concerns (although I won't go into detail as there is much too much information on that to cover here).

Suffice it to say, that turning the tap off and reaching for a glass of purified water, whether it be natural spring water or through reverse osmosis, is one of the healthiest and safest choices you could make for you and your family.

Natural spring water and water purified through reverse osmosis (RO) is largely free from contaminants that tend to find their way into the mass water supply. Natural spring water is of course water that is sourced naturally from springs and has not been polluted by other chemicals. A reverse osmosis process can remove impurities like fluoride, sediment and bacteria while retaining some beneficial health properties. The downside to RO is that it does remove healthy compounds like salt, manganese, iron and calcium. So, whenever possible, natural spring water should be your first choice.

Why Organic?

When fruits, vegetables and herbs are left alone and free to grow naturally from the earth, what you have are amazingly delicious and incredibly healthy food sources. Unfortunately, our world is not perfect, and we need to be aware of the potential health risks associated with eating foods that are genetically modified (as those found in most supermarkets). GMO's are now commonplace in our food culture, however there is research that indicates that GMO foods can be dangerous. The American Academy of Environmental Medicine for example, has warned of serious health risks after studies were made on GMO foods. Possible adverse effects of consuming GMO's include: allergic reactions for those with food allergies (from grafting genetic traits onto different crops), antibiotic resistance, decreased nutritional value, and exposure to pesticides.

But don't lose hope! While organic foods found at your local grocery store or farmer's market might be more expensive than the conventional fare, the increase in price is well worth the decrease in negative health effects. For those of us on a budget, you can also get a lot of usage out of one batch of fruit, since a pitcher of infused water can be reused and refilled for up to three days.

If possible, I would recommend that your ingredients be organic to maximize the health benefits of each recipe. If your budget does not allow for that, you will still at least benefit from the healthy dose vitamins and minerals contained in each recipe.

Purifying Waters

Delectable Detox

Rest & Digest

Clean Machine

Autumn's Arrival

Next Day Flush Away

Delectable Detox

Health Properties of this Recipe:

Young Coconut Water — has the same minerals / electrolytes as those found in your blood, improves blood circulation, energizes the body, relieves dehydration, addresses digestive disorders.

Young Coconut Meat — places good bacteria into the intestines, regulates digestion, aids in weight loss.

Cucumber — excellent source of B vitamins, hydrates the body, tightens skin, reduces water retention, replenishes essential nutrients, relieves headache.

Lime — stimulates the digestive system, increases digestive juices, relieves constipation, regulates sugar absorption, lowers blood pressure, eliminates bad cholesterol.

Delectable Detox

When your body can use a detox, your blood is on the top of the list. This infusion is perfect for a total system purification.

Ingredients:

- 1 Cup Fresh Young Coconut Water
- ½ Cup Fresh Coconut Meat
- ¼ Cucumber (sliced)
- 1 Lime (squeezed)
- ½ Cup strawberries (sliced)
- ½ Cup Blueberries
- ½ Tsp Non-Iodized Sea Salt
- 1 Liter Purified Water
- 1 Tsp Fresh Squeezed Lemon Juice (optional)

Directions: Mix up blueberries, strawberries, lime, coconut water and cucumber in a medium sized bowl and then pour into a pitcher. Fill with purified water, lemon juice and slowly stir in sea salt. Refrigerate for 5-6 hours. May be drunk at room temperature or with ice for a chilled beverage.

* Keep refrigerated and consume within 3 days

Strawberries — are rich in B-complex vitamins, anti-inflammatory, promote bone health, improve brain function, contain antioxidants.

Blueberries — one of the highest anti-oxidant fruits, lowers blood sugar levels and controls blood-glucose levels, includes vitamin A, E, C B-complex vitamins and minerals like manganese, copper, zinc and iron.

Sea Salt — helps with digestion, builds the immune system, improves skin health, improves sleep, contains trace minerals.

Rest and Digest

Health Properties of this Recipe:

Pears — are full of vitamins A, C, K, B2, B3 and B6, cleanse the colon, have plenty of minerals like calcium, magnesium, potassium, copper and manganese, also have boron needed to retain calcium in the body.

Mint — eliminates toxins in the body, soothes the digestive tract, deodorizes skin, cleanses the stomach, is anti-septic, whitens teeth.

Ginger — reduces flatulence, improves absorption of essential nutrients, relieves cramping and nausea.

Lemongrass — cleanses organs like the kidney, bladder, liver & pancreas, lowers cholesterol levels, combats high blood pressure.

Rest & Digest

Take this beverage when your digestive system needs a boost or a chance to release and rebuild.

Ingredients:

- 2 Cup Pears (sliced)
- 5-7 Sprigs Fresh Mint
- 3" Ginger (sliced or cubed)
- 1" Fresh or 1 Tbsp Dried Lemongrass
- 1 Tbsp Kefir (optional)
- ½ Tsp Non-Iodized Sea Salt
- 1 Liter Purified Water
- 1 Tsp Fresh Squeezed Lemon Juice (optional)

Directions: Stir together pears, mint, ginger, and lemongrass in a medium sized bowl and then pour into a pitcher. Fill with purified water, kefir, lemon juice and slowly stir in sea salt. Refrigerate for 5-6 hours. May be drunk at room temperature or with ice for a chilled beverage.

* Keep refrigerated and consume within 3 days

Kefir — cleanses the digestive tract, flushes bad bacteria from the intestines, relieves diarrhea, improves skin health.

Sea Salt — helps with digestion, builds the immune system, improves skin health, improves sleep, contains trace minerals.

Clean Machine

Health Properties of this Recipe:

Parsley — balance hormone levels, high source if iron, has more vitamin C than citrus.

Apples — help stop the absorption of negative cholesterol, chock full of phytonutrients and antioxidants, Counteract the negative effects of too much salt intake, help control blood pressure and heart rate.

Fennel — addresses any issues with indigestion or constipation, helps to promote eye health, great source of fiber, combats heart disease.

Hibiscus — maintains good blood pressure, keeps cholesterol levels in a healthy range.

Clean Machine

This infusion helps to cleanse your blood and purify your system. If you have a soft spot for sugar or salt and so experience an abnormal amount of water retention, this little recipe is a healthy way to flush out toxins that might be retained in your system.

Ingredients:

- 1 Cup Fennel (sliced)
- 1 Cup Apple (sliced)
- 1 Cup Pomegranate (sliced)
- 6 Sprigs Parsley
- 1 Tsp Hibiscus (fresh or dried)
- ½ Tsp Non-Iodized Sea Salt
- 1 Liter Purified Water
- 1 Tsp Fresh Squeezed Lemon Juice (optional)

Directions: Combine apple, pomegranate, parsley, fennel and hibiscus in a medium sized bowl and then pour into a pitcher. Fill with purified water, lemon juice and slowly stir in sea salt. Refrigerate for 5-6 hours. May be drunk at room temperature or with ice for a chilled beverage.

* Keep refrigerated and consume within 3 days

Pomegranate — promotes heart health, reduces arterial plaque, has plenty of antioxidants.

Sea Salt — helps with digestion, builds the immune system, improves skin health, improves sleep, contains trace minerals.

Autumn's Arrival

Health Properties of this Recipe:

Cinnamon Sticks — are anti-bacterial, neutralize bad odors, have anti-fungal properties, control blood sugar levels, relieve sore throat, relieve arthritic pain.

Apples — help stop the absorption of negative cholesterol, chock full of phytonutrients and antioxidants, Counteract the negative effects of too much salt intake, help control blood pressure and heart rate.

Cucumber — excellent source of B vitamins, hydrates the body, tightens skin, reduces water retention, replenishes essential nutrients, relieves headache.

Sea Salt — helps with digestion, builds the immune system, improves skin health, improves sleep, contains trace minerals.

Autumn's Arrival

I tend to drink this simple detoxifying infusion once Fall arrives. There's something about the crisp cool weather combined with the changing leaves that makes me reach for a glass of this cinnamon accented water every year.

Ingredients:

- 2 Cups Apple (thinly sliced)
- 2 Cinnamon Sticks
- ½ Cucumber (sliced)
- ½ Tsp Non-Iodized Sea Salt
- 1 Liter Purified Water
- 1 Tsp Fresh Squeezed Lemon Juice (optional)

Directions: Gently mix together apple, cinnamon sticks and cucumber in a medium sized bowl and then pour into a pitcher. Fill with purified water, lemon juice and slowly stir in sea salt. Refrigerate for 5-6 hours. May be drunk at room temperature or with ice for a chilled beverage.

* Keep refrigerated and consume within 3 days

Next Day Flush Away

Health Properties of this Recipe:

Star Fruit — relieve nausea and indigestion, are a good source of B-complex vitamins, contain a large quantity of vitamin c, have various minerals and electrolytes, are low in calories.

Blackberries — improve eyesight, are abundant in Vitamin C, contain ellagic acid which prevents skin damage from harmful UV rays, maintain blood sugar levels.

Lemons — are antiseptic, cleanse the blood, kidney & liver, help alkalize the body, high in mineral content, improve bowel function, can cure infection.

Sea Salt — helps with digestion, builds the immune system, improves skin health, improves sleep, contains trace minerals.

Next Day Flush Away

Sometimes we all indulge and let loose. A night out with some friends can occasionally result in one drink too many. This infusion will help refresh you the next morning and get you back into the swing of things.

Ingredients:

- 1 Cup Blackberry
- ½ Star Fruit (sliced)
- ½ Lemon (juiced)
- ½ Tsp Non-Iodized Sea Salt
- 1 Liter Purified Water

Directions: Gently mix together blackberries and star fruit in a medium sized bowl and then pour into a pitcher. Fill with purified water, lemon juice and slowly stir in sea salt. Refrigerate for 5-6 hours. May be drunk at room temperature or with ice for a chilled beverage.

* Keep refrigerated and consume within 3 days

Youthful Waters

Complexion Reflection

Timeless Tonic

Complexion Reflection

Health Properties of this Recipe:

Oranges — excellent source of Vitamin C, boost your immune system, help prevent Cancer by protecting the cells in your body. Oranges also contain collagen, which slows the skin's aging process, and also clears blemishes.

Mint — eliminates toxins in the body, soothes the digestive tract, deodorizes skin, cleanses the stomach, is anti-septic, whitens teeth.

Cucumber — excellent source of B vitamins, hydrates the body, tightens skin, reduces water retention, replenishes essential nutrients, relieves headache.

Sea Salt — helps with digestion, builds the immune system, improves skin health, improves sleep, contains trace minerals.

Complexion Reflection

It's nice to have infusions that address a number of different health issues all at once. Sometimes though you just have a specific goal in mind – like skin health. This infusion is tailored specifically for those wishing to improve the look and feel of their skin. It's delicious, simple, and it works!

Ingredients:

- 4-6 Mint leaves
- ¼ Cucumber (sliced)
- 2 Cups Oranges (sliced)
- ½ Tsp Non-Iodized Sea Salt
- 1 Liter Purified Water
- 1 Tsp Fresh Squeezed Lemon Juice (optional)

Directions: Gently mix together cucumber, orange and mint in a medium sized bowl and then pour into a pitcher. Fill with purified water, lemon juice and slowly stir in sea salt. Refrigerate for 5-6 hours. May be drunk at room temperature or with ice for a chilled beverage.

* Keep refrigerated and consume within 3 days

Timeless Tonic

Health Properties of this Recipe:

Pineapple — loaded with vitamins and minerals, prevents cough and loosens mucus, promotes healthy gums, improves bone health, provides arthritic relief, aids in digestion.

Watermelon — improves arterial health, has high levels of antioxidants, reduces blood pressure, regulates blood sugar levels.

Basil — prevents premature aging, high antioxidant levels, is antibacterial, treats indigestion and constipation, high in magnesium which improves blood flow.

Sea Salt — helps with digestion, builds the immune system, improves skin health, improves sleep, contains trace minerals.

Timeless Tonic

For those searching for the fountain of youth, look no further! This simple drink will slow down the hands of time while letting you enjoy the ride.

Ingredients:

- 1 Cup pineapple (cubed)
- 2 Cups watermelon (cubed)
- 6-8 Basil Leaves
- ½ Tsp Non-Iodized Sea Salt
- 1 Liter Purified Water
- 1 Tsp Fresh Squeezed Lemon Juice (optional)

Directions: Gently mix together pineapple, watermelon and basil leaves in a medium sized bowl and then pour into a pitcher. Fill with purified water, lemon juice and slowly stir in sea salt. Refrigerate for 5-6 hours. May be drunk at room temperature or with ice for a chilled beverage.

* Keep refrigerated and consume within 3 days

Rejuvenating Waters

Regeneration Elation

Ravishing Repair

Alive and Thrive

Slice of life

Regeneration Elation

Health Properties of this Recipe:

Blueberries — one of the highest antioxidant fruits, lowers blood sugar levels and controls blood-glucose levels, includes vitamin A, E, C, B-complex vitamins and minerals like manganese, copper, zinc and iron.

Oranges — excellent source of Vitamin C, boost your immune system, help prevent Cancer by protecting the cells in your body.

Parsley — balance hormone levels, high source if iron, has more vitamin C than citrus.

Kiwi — loaded with Vitamin C, Vitamin E, potassium and magnesium, helps with weight loss, and improves sleep.

Regeneration Elation

For anyone who suffers from sleep deprivation, poor diet or stress, this infusion will help get you back on your feet.

Ingredients:

- ½ Cup Peaches (sliced)
- 1 Cup Blueberries
- ½ Cup Kiwi (sliced)
- 1 Cup Oranges (sliced)
- 6 Sprigs Parsley
- ½ Tsp Non-Iodized Sea Salt
- 1 Liter Purified Water
- 1 Tsp Fresh Squeezed Lemon Juice (optional)

Directions: Gently mix together peaches, blueberries, kiwi, oranges and parsley in a medium sized bowl and then pour into a pitcher. Fill with purified water, lemon juice and slowly stir in sea salt. Refrigerate for 5-6 hours. May be drunk at room temperature or with ice for a chilled beverage.

* Keep refrigerated and consume within 3 days

Peaches — contain 10 different vitamins with lots of Vitamin C (an antioxidant), loaded with potassium to help with blood pressure and prevent kidney stones.

Sea Salt — helps with digestion, builds the immune system, improves skin health, improves sleep, contains trace minerals.

Ravishing Repair

Health Properties of this Recipe:

Cantaloupe — is a good source of folate which prevents anemia, contains carotenoids which decrease the risk of cancer and cardiovascular disease, is rich in vitamin C which repairs tissue, contains potassium which is an electrolyte (aids in muscle and heart health).

Carrots — are chocked full of vitamin A, prevent heart disease and strokes, are a wonderful antioxidant source, promote healthy vision.

Ginger — fights bacterial infections, is anti-inflammatory, is a pain reliever, can kill Cancer cells, relieves menstrual pain, prevents heart-attacks, relieves nausea.

Ravishing Repair

There are many ways in which we can heal our bodies after going through a strenuous physical event (whatever that may be). In such an instance, you can take this infusion to help aid in your body's healing process.

Ingredients:

- ¼ Cup Carrots (sliced)
- 1 Cup Apple (sliced)
- 2 Cups Cantaloupe (cubed)
- 1" Fresh Ginger (sliced)
- ½ Tsp Non-Iodized Sea Salt
- 1 Liter Purified Water
- 1 Tsp Fresh Squeezed Lemon Juice (optional)

Directions: Gently mix together carrots, apple, cantaloupe and ginger in a medium sized bowl and then pour into a pitcher. Fill with purified water, lemon juice and slowly stir in sea salt. Refrigerate for 5-6 hours. May be drunk at room temperature or with ice for a chilled beverage.

* Keep refrigerated and consume within 3 days

Apples — help stop the absorption of negative cholesterol, chock full of phytonutrients and antioxidants, Counteract the negative effects of too much salt intake, help control blood pressure and heart rate.

Sea Salt — helps with digestion, builds the immune system, improves skin health, improves sleep, contains trace minerals.

Alive and Thrive

Health Properties of this Recipe:

Grapefruit — contain lycopene which prevents cell aging, boosts good HDL cholesterol and lowers bad LDL Cholesterol, combats colds, prevents arthritis.

Oranges — excellent source of Vitamin C, boost your immune system, help prevent Cancer by protecting the cells in your body.

Cucumber — excellent source of B vitamins, hydrates the body, tightens skin, reduces water retention, replenishes essential nutrients, relieves headache.

Alive and Thrive

Sometimes it's nice to be given a refreshing reminder that we are a living, breathing, thriving, pulsating work of nature's art – and isn't it wonderful to find that reminder in a glass! This infusion is a fresh and fun way to widen those eyes and bring a smile to your face.

Ingredients:

- ½ Cup Grapefruit (sliced)
- 2 Cups Orange (sliced)
- ½ Cucumber, sliced
- 4-6 Mint Leaves
- ½ Tsp Non-Iodized Sea Salt
- 1 Liter Purified Water
- 1 Tsp Fresh Squeezed Lemon Juice (optional)

Directions: Gently mix together grapefruit, oranges, cucumber and mint leaves in a medium sized bowl and then pour into a pitcher. Fill with purified water, lemon juice and slowly stir in sea salt. Refrigerate for 5-6 hours. May be drunk at room temperature or with ice for a chilled beverage.

* Keep refrigerated and consume within 3 days

Mint — eliminates toxins in the body, soothes the digestive tract, deodorizes skin, cleanses the stomach, is anti-septic, whitens teeth.

Sea Salt — helps with digestion, builds the immune system, improves skin health, improves sleep, contains trace minerals.

Slice of Life

Health Properties of this Recipe:

Lychees — contain high levels of Vitamin C, are anti-fungal, are full of Calcium which promote healthy teeth and bones, lower the risk of heart disease.

Lemons — are antiseptic, cleanse the blood, kidney & liver, help alkalize the body, high in mineral content, improve bowel function, can cure infection.

Mint — eliminates toxins in the body, soothes the digestive tract, deodorizes skin, cleanses the stomach, is anti-septic, whitens teeth.

Slice of Life

This is one of those powerhouse infusions that assists with the total functioning of the body. Take this when you feel sluggish or even when you feel fine, the properties of this drink make it worthwhile any time.

Ingredients:

- 2 Cups Raspberries
- 1 Lemon (sliced)
- 6 Mint Sprigs
- 2-3 Lychees (sliced)
- ½ Tsp Non-Iodized Sea Salt
- 1 Liter Purified Water
- 1 Tsp Fresh Squeezed Lemon Juice (optional)

Directions: Gently mix together raspberries, lemon, lychees and mint leaves in a medium sized bowl and then pour into a pitcher. Fill with purified water, lemon juice and slowly stir in sea salt. Refrigerate for 5-6 hours. May be drunk at room temperature or with ice for a chilled beverage.

* Keep refrigerated and consume within 3 days

Raspberries — help manage blood sugar levels, are a good source of phytonutrients and antioxidants, improves bowel function, prevents vaginal infections.

Sea Salt — helps with digestion, builds the immune system, improves skin health, improves sleep, contains trace minerals.

Athletic Waters

Sporty Serenade

Radical Replenish

Marvelous Maintenance

Rise and Recharge

Sporty Serenade

Health Properties of this Recipe:

Blueberries — one of the highest antioxidant fruits, lowers blood sugar levels and controls blood-glucose levels, includes vitamin A, E, C, B-complex vitamins and minerals like manganese, copper, zinc and iron.

Young Coconut Water — has the same minerals / electrolytes as those found in your blood, improves blood circulation, energizes the body, relieves dehydration, addresses digestive disorders.

Dates — boost energy levels, manage blood sugar levels, improve heart health, relieves constipation and diarrhea.

Sporty Serenade

There's nothing better than breaking a sweat and feeling pampered afterwards. After a long afternoon at the gym, you can enjoy this sweet little recipe for its revitalizing properties and relaxing after effects.

Ingredients:

- 3 Cups of Coconut Water
- ½ Cup Mango
- 1 Cup of Blueberries
- 1 Cup of Purified Water
- 1/8 Teaspoon of Sea Salt
- 2 Dates

Directions: In a blender combine coconut water, mango, blueberries, dates, water and sea salt. Blend until smooth. Chill for 4-6 hours, or add ice and enjoy.

* Keep refrigerated and consume within 3 days

Mango — encourages eye and skin health, increases sex drive, promotes healthy teeth and gums, boosts the immune system.

Sea Salt — helps with digestion, builds the immune system, improves skin health, improves sleep, contains trace minerals.

Radical Replenish

Health Properties of this Recipe:

Pomegranate Seeds — low in calories, high in vitamins, good for Cancer prevention, promotes heart health.

Pineapple — loaded with vitamins and minerals, prevents cough and loosens mucus, promotes healthy gums, improves bone health, provides arthritic relief, aids in digestion.

Cherries — reduce muscle inflammation, improve weight management, reduce chances of stroke, improve sleep

Sea Salt — helps with digestion, builds the immune system, improves skin health, improves sleep, contains trace minerals.

Radical Replenish

For those of us who like to be physically active, this infusion will help replenish your energy reserves and get you ready for that next marathon (whatever that may look like!).

Ingredients:

- ½ Pomegranate Seeds
- 1 Cup Pineapple (cubed)
- 1 Cup Cherries (pitted)
- ½ Tsp Non-Iodized Sea Salt
- 1 Liter Purified Water
- 1 Tsp Fresh Squeezed Lemon Juice (optional)

Directions: Combine Pomegranate Seeds, Pineapple and Cherries in a medium sized bowl and then pour into a pitcher. Fill with purified water, lemon juice and slowly stir in sea salt. Refrigerate for 5-6 hours. May be drunk at room temperature or with ice for a chilled beverage.

* Keep refrigerated and consume within 3 days

Marvelous Maintenance

Health Properties of this Recipe:

Ginger — fights bacterial infections, is anti-inflammatory, is a pain reliever, can kill Cancer cells, relieves menstrual pain, prevents heart-attacks, relieves nausea.

Pineapple — loaded with vitamins and minerals, prevents cough and loosens mucus, promotes healthy gums, improves bone health, provides arthritic relief, aids in digestion.

Lime — stimulates the digestive system, increases digestive juices, relieves constipation, regulates sugar absorption, lowers blood pressure, eliminates bad cholesterol.

Marvelous Maintenance

If work or extra activities have been wearing your body out, this infusion will help bring you back into balance. Sometimes all you need is a pick-me-up, and this is it!

Ingredients:

- 3 Cups Pineapple (sliced or cubed)
- Thinly Sliced Ginger (5 slices)
- Lime (sliced)
- 10- 12 Mint Leaves
- ½ Tsp Non-Iodized Sea Salt
- 1 Liter Purified Water
- 1 Tsp Fresh Squeezed Lemon Juice (optional)

Directions: Gently mix together pineapple, ginger and mint leaves in a medium sized bowl and then pour into a pitcher. Fill with purified water, lime juice, lemon juice and slowly stir in sea salt. Refrigerate for 5-6 hours. May be drunk at room temperature or with ice for a chilled beverage.

* Keep refrigerated and consume within 3 days

Mint — eliminates toxins in the body, soothes the digestive tract, deodorizes skin, cleanses the stomach, is anti-septic, whitens teeth.

Sea Salt — helps with digestion, builds the immune system, improves skin health, improves sleep, contains trace minerals.

Rise and Recharge

Health Properties of this Recipe:

Pineapple — loaded with vitamins and minerals, prevents cough and loosens mucus, promotes healthy gums, improves bone health, provides arthritic relief, aids in digestion.

Lemons — are antiseptic, cleanse the blood, kidney & liver, help alkalize the body, high in mineral content, improve bowel function, can cure infection.

Oranges — excellent source of Vitamin C, boost your immune system, help prevent Cancer by protecting the cells in your body.

Rise and Recharge

Most of us are not professional athletes, but sometimes we do take our bodies to extremes. When that happens, it's much better to turn to a homemade infusion than commercially made sports drinks. After a morning workout, you can replace your body's electrolytes with this easy, fun and delicious recipe.

Ingredients:

- 2 Dates
- ½ Cup Pineapple (chopped)
- ¼ Cup Freshly Squeezed Lemon Juice
- ½ Cup Freshly Squeezed Orange Juice
- 1 ½ to 2 Cups Purified Water
- 1/8 Teaspoon of Sea Salt

Directions: In a blender combine pineapple, dates, lemon juice, orange juice, water and sea salt. Blend until smooth. Chill for 4-6 hours, or add ice and enjoy.

* Keep refrigerated and consume within 3 days

Sea Salt — helps with digestion, builds the immune system, improves skin health, improves sleep, contains trace minerals.

Dates — boost energy levels, manage blood sugar levels, improve heart health, relieves constipation and diarrhea.

KATE EVANS SCOTT & DAVID PEARSON

Sparkling Waters

Ruby Relief

Peachy Keen

Perfect Pick-Me-Up

Beautiful Boost

Super Strength

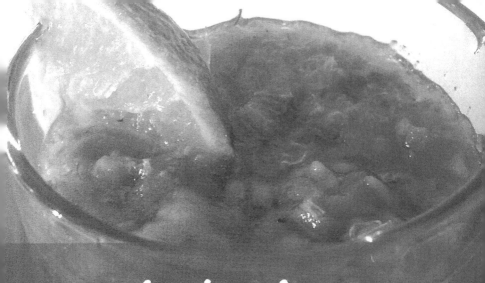

Ruby Relief

Health Properties of this Recipe:

Raspberries — help manage blood sugar levels, are a good source of phytonutrients and antioxidants, improves bowel function, prevents vaginal infections.

Dates — boost energy levels, manage blood sugar levels, improve heart health, relieves constipation and diarrhea.

Lime — stimulates the digestive system, increases digestive juices, relieves constipation, regulates sugar absorption, lowers blood pressure, eliminates bad cholesterol.

Ruby Relief

This sparkling refreshment is one that will leave you feeling balanced and vibrant. It's blood sugar regulating properties make it a good choice for those monitoring their levels.

Ingredients:

- 2 Cups Raspberries
- 1 Lime (juiced)
- 4 Dates
- 3-5 Cups Sparkling Mineral Water
- Ice

Directions: Blend raspberries in a blender. Strain with a fine strainer if desired to make drink smoother. Next add lime juice and dates to the raspberry puree and blend well. Put mixture into a pitcher and add sparkling mineral water. Chill for 4-6 hours if desired or consume immediately.

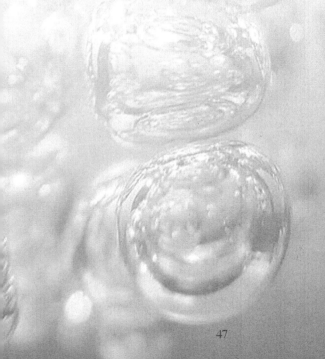

Peachy Keen

Health Properties of this Recipe:

Dates — boost energy levels, manage blood sugar levels, improve heart health, relieves constipation and diarrhea.

Pineapple — loaded with vitamins and minerals, prevents cough and loosens mucus, promotes healthy gums, improves bone health, provides arthritic relief, aids in digestion.

Ginger — fights bacterial infections, is anti-inflammatory, is a pain reliever, can kill Cancer cells, relieves menstrual pain, prevents heart-attacks, relieves nausea.

Peachy Keen

Who doesn't love a little wow in their water? This sparkling mixture is full of goodness and zing – just the right combination of strong and subtle flavors!

Ingredients:

- 4-6 Peaches (about 1 ½ cups pureed)
- 1 Tbsp Lime Juice
- 1 Cup Pineapple
- 1-2 Tsp Grated Ginger (more to taste)
- 4 Dates
- 3-5 Cups Sparkling Mineral Water

Directions: Pit the peach and blend in a blender. Strain with a fine strainer if desired to make drink smoother. Next add lime juice, dates and grated ginger to the peach mix and blend well. Put mixture into a pitcher and add sparkling mineral water. Chill for 4-6 hours if desired or consume immediately.

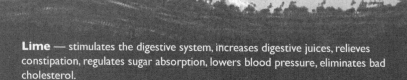

Lime — stimulates the digestive system, increases digestive juices, relieves constipation, regulates sugar absorption, lowers blood pressure, eliminates bad cholesterol.

Peaches — contain 10 different vitamins with lots of vitamin C (an antioxidant), loaded with potassium to help with blood pressure and prevent kidney stones.

Perfect Pick-Me-Up

Health Properties of this Recipe:

Pineapple — loaded with vitamins and minerals, prevents cough and loosens mucus, promotes healthy gums, improves bone health, provides arthritic relief, aids in digestion.

Lemons — are antiseptic, cleanse the blood, kidney & liver, help alkalize the body, high in mineral content, improve bowel function, can cure infection.

Dates — boost energy levels, manage blood sugar levels, improve heart health, relieves constipation and diarrhea.

Perfect Pick-Me-Up

Get well in style! This sparkling infusion has all of the things you need to recover from the flu or general malaise – the sparkling water enlivens the taste buds and then brings home the goods with a tangy twist.

Ingredients:

- 2 Cup Pineapple
- 1 Lemon (juiced)
- 4 Dates
- 3-5 Cups Sparkling Mineral Water
- Ice

Directions: Blend pineapple in a blender. Strain with a fine strainer if desired to make drink smoother. Next add dates and lemon juice to the pineapple puree and blend well. Put mixture into a pitcher and add sparkling mineral water. Chill for 4-6 hours if desired or consume immediately.

Beautiful Boost

Health Properties of this Recipe:

Oranges — excellent source of Vitamin C, boost your immune system, help prevent Cancer by protecting the cells in your body.

Blackberries — improve eyesight, are abundant in Vitamin C, contain ellagic acid which prevents skin damage from harmful UV rays, maintain blood sugar levels.

Dates — boost energy levels, manage blood sugar levels, improve heart health, relieves constipation and diarrhea.

Beautiful Boost

This infusion will help to enhance your natural beauty - inside and out. It's full of properties that improve the look and feel of your body. A youthful revival!

Ingredients:

- 1 Cup Blackberries
- 2 Cup Orange (sliced)
- 4 Dates
- 3-5 Cups Sparkling Mineral Water
- Ice

Directions: Blend blackberries and orange in a blender. Strain with a fine strainer if desired to make drink smoother. Next add dates to the orange blackberry puree and blend well. Put mixture into a pitcher and add sparkling mineral water. Chill for 4-6 hours if desired or consume immediately.

Super Strength

Health Properties of this Recipe:

Strawberries — are rich in B-complex vitamins, anti-inflammatory, promote bone health, improve brain function, contains antioxidants.

Peaches — contain 10 different vitamins with lots of vitamin C (an antioxidant), loaded with potassium to help with blood pressure and prevent kidney stones.

Dates — boost energy levels, manage blood sugar levels, improve heart health, relieves constipation and diarrhea.

Super Strength

Reach for this infusion to improve your core strength and prevent toxins from building up in your system. What a delicious way to promote a healthy future!

Ingredients:

- 1 Cup Strawberries
- 2 Cup Peaches
- 4 Dates
- 3-5 Cups Sparkling Mineral Water
- Ice

Directions: Pit peach, then blend peach and strawberries in a blender. Strain with a fine strainer if desired to make drink smoother. Next add dates to the peach strawberry puree and blend well. Put mixture into a pitcher and add sparkling mineral water. Chill for 4-6 hours if desired or consume immediately.

Blissful Waters

Recollection Reverie

Sweet Sublime

Calming Connection

Worry-Free Remedy

Fruitful Flirtation

Sleep Serene

Recollection Reverie

Health Properties of this Recipe:

Blueberries — one of the highest antioxidant fruits, lowers blood sugar levels and controls blood-glucose levels, includes vitamin A, E, C, B-complex vitamins and minerals like manganese, copper, zinc and iron.

Apples — help stop the absorption of negative cholesterol, chock full of phytonutrients and antioxidants, Counteract the negative effects of too much salt intake, help control blood pressure and heart rate.

Rosemary — contains carnosol which researchers have found to have profound cancer fighting properties, combats headache, improves memory, is an immune system booster, aids in digestion.

Oranges — excellent source of Vitamin C, boost your immune system, help prevent Cancer by protecting the cells in your body.

Recollection Reverie

I'm of the belief that time travel is possible – at least, with this infusion in hand. Every time I drink this recipe I find myself thinking back to my childhood when I was care-free and full of wonder. This infusion is a time-machine of sorts; let it transport you to that special place inside of yourself that remembers those wonder years!

Ingredients:

- ½ Cup Blueberry
- ½ Cup Apple (sliced)
- 3 Sprigs Rosemary
- 1 Cup Orange (sliced)
- ½ Cup Blackberry
- ½ Lime (squeezed)
- ½ Tsp Non-Iodized Sea Salt
- 1 Liter Purified Water
- 1 Tsp Fresh Squeezed Lemon Juice (optional)

Directions: Gently mix together blueberries, apple, orange, blackberries, and rosemary in a medium sized bowl and then pour into a pitcher. Fill with purified water, lime juice, lemon juice and slowly stir in sea salt. Refrigerate for 5-6 hours. May be drunk at room temperature or with ice for a chilled beverage.

* Keep refrigerated and consume within 3 days

Blackberries — improve eyesight, are abundant in Vitamin C, contain ellagic acid which prevents skin damage from harmful UV rays, maintain blood sugar levels.

Lime — stimulates the digestive system, increases digestive juices, relieves constipation, regulates sugar absorption, lowers blood pressure, eliminates bad cholesterol.

Sea Salt — helps with digestion, builds the immune system, improves skin health, improves sleep, contains trace minerals.

Sweet Sublime

Health Properties of this Recipe:

Mint — eliminates toxins in the body, soothes the digestive tract, deodorizes skin, cleanses the stomach, is anti-septic, whitens teeth.

Oranges — excellent source of Vitamin C, boost your immune system, help prevent Cancer by protecting the cells in your body.

Lemongrass — cleanses organs like the kidney, bladder, liver & pancreas, lowers cholesterol levels, combats high blood pressure.

Sweet Sublime

This is one of my favorite infusions. The simple sweetness from the vanilla bean and citrus-mint flavor always makes me want to kick my feet up and say "Ahhh"... perfect for unwinding.

Ingredients:

- 1 Large Stalk Lemongrass, Chopped & Crushed (a little)
- ¼ Cup Fresh Mint Leaves
- ½ Large Vanilla Bean, Sliced Lengthwise
- 2 Cups Orange, Sliced
- ½ Tsp Non-Iodized Sea Salt
- 1 Liter Purified Water
- 1 Tsp Fresh Squeezed Lemon Juice (optional)

Directions: Gently mix together lemongrass, mint leaves, vanilla bean and oranges in a medium sized bowl and then pour into a pitcher. Fill with purified water, lemon juice and slowly stir in sea salt. Refrigerate for 5-6 hours. May be drunk at room temperature or with ice for a chilled beverage.

* Keep refrigerated and consume within 3 days

Vanilla Bean — regulates metabolism, assists the nervous system, contains minerals like calcium and magnesium, considered to be an aphrodisiac.

Sea Salt — helps with digestion, builds the immune system, improves skin health, improves sleep, contains trace minerals.

Calming Connection

Health Properties of this Recipe:

Lavender — relieves anxiety and tension, improves sleep, soothes nerves, relaxes muscles, relieves irritated skin, naturally antiseptic.

Blueberries — one of the highest anti-oxidant fruits, lowers blood sugar levels and controls blood-glucose levels, includes vitamin A, E, C, B-complex vitamins and minerals like manganese, copper, zinc and iron.

Young Coconut Water — has the same minerals / electrolytes as those found in your blood, improves blood circulation, energizes the body, relieves dehydration, addresses digestive disorders.

Calming Connection

Make this infusion when you've had a long day or just need to take a load off of your shoulders. Everyone has those moments when life feels a little overwhelming, so this drink can help bring things back into perspective.

Ingredients:

- 2 Sprigs Lavender (fresh) or 1 ½ Tsp Dried
- 1 Cup Blueberries
- 1 Cup Young Coconut Water
- 1 Cup Raspberries
- ½ Tsp Non-Iodized Sea Salt
- 1 Liter Purified Water
- 1 Tsp Fresh Squeezed Lemon Juice (optional)

Directions: Add ingredients to a large pitcher. Release the juices in the mixture by gently pressing on them with a spatula. Add ice cubes on top (to weigh the mixture down and then fill with purified water). Refrigerate 5-6 hours.

* Keep refrigerated and consume within 3 days

Raspberries — help manage blood sugar levels, are a good source of phytonutrients and antioxidants, improves bowel function, prevents vaginal infections.

Sea Salt — helps with digestion, builds the immune system, improves skin health, improves sleep, contains trace minerals.

Worry-Free Remedy

Health Properties of this Recipe:

Nutmeg — relieves fatigue and stress, reduces anxiety and depression, relieves abdominal pain, reduces inflammation, addresses digestion problems, cleanses the liver and kidney.

Rose Hips — huge source of vitamin C, are also a good source for vitamin A, B and E, contain zinc, selenium, calcium, manganese and iron.

Lemongrass — cleanses organs like the kidney, bladder, liver & pancreas, lowers cholesterol levels, combats high blood pressure.

Cinnamon Sticks — are anti-bacterial, neutralize bad odors, have anti-fungal properties, control blood sugar levels, relieve sore throat, relieve arthritic pain.

Worry-Free Remedy

This infusion can be served hot or cold. It's so full of cleansing and revitalizing properties that this may be the only infusion you'll ever drink! Alternatively, you can save this one for those days when it seems like nothing is going right – this will definitely help lift your spirits.

Ingredients:

- 4 tablespoons rose hips
- 1 tablespoon lemongrass (dried)
- 1 cinnamon stick
- 1 whole nutmeg
- 1 teaspoon hibiscus flowers
- 1 teaspoon fennel seed
- ½ teaspoon orange peel (dried)
- 4 cups filtered water
- Ice (optional)
- Raw honey or fresh fruit juice (optional)

Directions: Mix dried ingredients and place in a tightly sealed glass container. Next - boil water in a pot on the stove or in a tea kettle. Once boiled, remove from heat and add 3-5 tablespoons of the mixture to the water. Cover to maintain all the nutritional benefits so they aren't lost through the steam. Allow to steep for 40 minutes. Strain and then sweeten with honey to taste. If you wish to drink this cold, place it covered in the fridge until cold, and then drink chilled or with ice. Store extra tea in the fridge for 5-7 days.

Hibiscus — maintains good blood pressure, keeps cholesterol levels in a healthy range.

Fennel — addresses any issues with indigestion or constipation, helps to promote eye health, great source of fiber, combats heart disease.

Orange Peel — excellent source of vitamin C, boost your immune system, help prevent Cancer by protecting the cells in your body.

Fruitful Flirtation

Health Properties of this Recipe:

Cardamom — improves blood circulation, relieves respiratory allergies, heals urinary tract infections, improves digestion.

Mango — encourages eye and skin health, increases sex drive, promotes healthy teeth and gums, boosts the immune system.

Vanilla Bean — regulates metabolism, assists the nervous system, contains minerals like calcium and magnesium, considered to be an aphrodisiac.

Fruitful Flirtation

This little recipe has a bit of sassy thrown into the mix. The result of consuming this infusion makes it a beverage you'll want to share with your partner on a romantic evening!

Ingredients:

- 2 Cups Orange (sliced)
- 1 Tablespoon Cardamom
- ½ Large Vanilla Bean (sliced lengthwise)
- 1 Mango (chopped)
- ½ Tsp Non-Iodized Sea Salt
- 1 Liter Purified Water
- 1 Tsp Fresh Squeezed Lemon Juice (optional)

Directions: Gently mix together orange, cardamom, vanilla bean and mango in a medium sized bowl and then pour into a pitcher. Fill with purified water, lemon juice and slowly stir in sea salt. Refrigerate for 5-6 hours. May be drunk at room temperature or with ice for a chilled beverage.

* Keep refrigerated and consume within 3 days

Oranges — excellent source of Vitamin C, boost your immune system, help prevent Cancer by protecting the cells in your body.

Sea Salt — helps with digestion, builds the immune system, improves skin health, improves sleep, contains trace minerals.

Sleep Serene

Health Properties of this Recipe:

Lemons — are antiseptic, cleanse the blood, kidney & liver, help alkalize the body, high in mineral content, improve bowel function, can cure infection.

Pears — are full of vitamins A, C, K, B2, B3 and B6, cleanse the colon, have plenty of minerals like calcium, magnesium, potassium, copper and manganese, also have boron needed to retain calcium in the body.

Cherries — reduce muscle inflammation, improve weight management, reduce chances of stroke, improve sleep.

Kiwi — loaded with Vitamin C, Vitamin E, potassium and magnesium, helps with weight loss, and improves sleep.

Sleep Serene

When a good night's sleep is long overdue, take this infusion a few hours before bed. You'll find it easier to rest your mind and drift off into a blissful place.

Ingredients:

- ½ Lemon (sliced)
- ½ Cup Cherries (pitted)
- 1 Pear (sliced)
- 1 Kiwi (sliced)
- 5 Sprigs Cilantro
- ½ Tsp Non-Iodized Sea Salt
- 1 Liter Purified Water
- 1 Tsp Fresh Squeezed Lemon Juice (optional)

Directions: Gently mix together lemon, cherries, pear, kiwi and cilantro in a medium sized bowl and then pour into a pitcher. Fill with purified water, lemon juice and slowly stir in sea salt. Refrigerate for 5-6 hours. May be drunk at room temperature or with ice for a chilled beverage.

* Keep refrigerated and consume within 3 days

Cilantro — assists the digestive system, treats salmonella poisoning, can relieve the common cold, reduces bad LDL cholesterol and increases good HDL cholesterol, prevents skin cancer.

Sea Salt — helps with digestion, builds the immune system, improves skin health, improves sleep, contains trace minerals.

About The Authors

Kate Evans Scott is a stay-at-home mom to a preschooler and a toddler. In her former life she worked in graphic design and publishing which she now draws from to create inspiring books for young children and parents.

Her passion for writing began with her preschooler who is an encyclopedia of all things animal, vegetable and mineral. With a deep interest to create books that satisfy his desire to learn, and his love of food, Kids Love Press was born.

David Pearson has over 10 years experience in emergency and survival training from the oil and gas industry. He left his field after witnessing the startling devastation and impact that drilling is taking on our planet, its communities and natural resources.

His greatest passion is being outdoors and learning new ways to tread lightly. He lives on a homestead in Oregon with his wife, two children and his dog Ernie.

More By Kate Evans Scott:

Available Now on Amazon

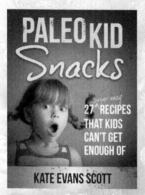

Available Now on Amazon

Available Now on Amazon

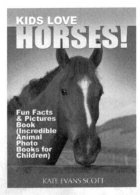

Available Now on Amazon

Available Now on Amazon

More By David Pearson:

Available Now on Amazon

NOTES

NOTES

NOTES

6751291R00046

Made in the USA
San Bernardino, CA
14 December 2013